Hope, Love and The Lack Thereof

An Evolution of Mind

Poems by
REESE LANDRY

Copyright © 2025 Reese Landry

Published in the United States of America by the Brooklyn Writers Press, an imprint of Book Biz Hub, LLC

brooklynwriterspress.com

The Brooklyn Writers Press values and protects copyright as the foundation of our literary community. Thank you for purchasing an authorized edition of this work and for respecting intellectual property laws by not reproducing, scanning, or distributing any part of it without permission. Your support enables our authors to continue creating meaningful work and allows the Brooklyn Writers Press to maintain our mission of producing award-winning, visually stunning, and expertly crafted books across fiction, poetry, non-fiction, and beyond. Together, we're building a literary community that values authenticity, artistry, and the transformative power of books.

In accordance with Article 4(3) of the Digital Single Market Directive 2019/790, the Brooklyn Writers Press expressly reserves this work from the text and data mining exception.

For permissions or information on bulk orders:
contact@bklynwriterspress.com

ISBNs:
978-1-952991-44-8 (e-Book)
978-1-952991-45-5 (Paperback)
978-1-952991-46-2 (Hardback)

Library of Congress No. 2025909774

First Edition

Cover design by Sonnie Wing

Interior Design by the Brooklyn Writers Press

Contents

HOPE

My First (Good) Poem 14

Ten Paces and Turn 15

Woodsy 16

Writing Minds 17

Life is Poetry is Life 18

Thoughts, Judgment, and Lucidity 19

Afterlife at Sea 20

Half-Hopes 21

Maybe I Should Start Charging Late Fees 22

The Curse of Caring 24

A Typewriter Reality 25

An Old Mantra 26

The Sad Child's Sacrifice 27

Fight or Flight or Freeze 28

With Water 29

Imperfect Porcelain 30

Peace of Mind Hides in The Acceptance of Our Sorrows 31

Red Lenses 32

Hell Is 33

Over The Years 34

In Memory of Skyla Alves 35

Enough 36

Lessons 37

Regrets 38

Unrecovered 39

Choosing 40

My First Performance 41

LOVE

The Treasured Queen 44

What is Love? 46

A Rose 47

Lost Constellations 48

Picking Petals 49

"This" and "That" 50

The Musician and The Poet 51

Love Bomb! 52

No One's Watching 53

Eyes In the Sun 54

What Hearts Are Meant For 55

Broad Silhouettes 56

Entirely, Eternally 57

Our First Home 58

More of You 59

The Sweetest of Dreams 60

When The Stars Lived With Us 61

All the Little Things 63

Sunken Footsteps 64

From Smoke to Water 65

The Suppliant 66

Between Us 67

Watch the Sky 68

The Third Moon 69

A Covetous Heart 70

All Your Hearts 71

My Love 72

The Secret of the Sea 73

An Ode to Those Loved Only in Their Dreams 74

Close Your Eyes 76

I Thought with The Butterflies and It Was the Death of Me 77

Beneath the Sea 78

The Mirror 79

The Princess Who Loves the Peasant 80

Ninety Percent 81

Should Be 82

Woman vs. Wind 83

To Beg 84

In The Landing 85

In So Many Words 86

Multiple Choices 87

Insecure 88

Without Me 89

Mortar Seals 91

The Thirst 92

Days Sober 94

His Frozen Throne 95

Blackened Bridges 98

We Were Made with Two Hands So We Could Hold Our Own When We're Alone 99

I Called to You from the Caveside and I Waited 100

When You Let Her Go 102

A Love Letter 103

Don't Stop 104

Hot Air Balloon Love 105

Freer 106

The Root of All Happiness 107

The Root of All Unhappiness 108
The Other Cheek 109
And Maybe the First 110
A Lonely Bird 111
Poison Blood 112
The Child 113
Fitting 114
Lunar Tears 115
The Isle 116
The Shadow of a Doubt 117
Hospice for Broken Hearts 118
More Love 119
A Song 120
What I Love Most About You 122
The Birds' Window 123
Hints & Traces 124
True and Real 125
Gatsby's Green Light 126
The Wordsmith 127

The Lack Thereof

What No One Understands About Clinical Depression 130
The Weight 131
Diamond's Blood 132
My Demons & I 133
Either Or 134
All-Intrusive 135
The Falling Water 136
The Midas Touch 137
Voluntary Confinement 138

No Doubt 139
Who is She? 140
I Hate the Word "I" 141
I Apologize 142
Why Am I Crying? 143
The Heat 144
Senseless 145
What is That Sound? 146
Crossing 147
Gaps 148
Pieced Together 149
The Tunnel 150
Flashing Lights 151
To Pursue 152
What Are You Writing For? 153
A Haiku for My Son 155

*For Mr. Bruckner and Mrs. Fish, my father
and stepmother, my sisters, my abuela.*

*For Jonah Durant, without whom
this book would not exist.*

*For my mother, Ana Landry, without whom
I would not exist.*

For my son, Buggo, for whom I persist.

*In loving memory of Abuelo Zeke, Uncle Alfred,
Grandpa Chuck, Nana Phyllis and Grandpa Paul.*

A Book
*You could fill a book
with the things I don't know.
But I filled this one
with the things I do.*

HOPE

To have hope
To lose hope
To find hope again

My First (Good) Poem

Amazing and beautiful,
they'll take you on an adventure.
So, lie out on your porch at night
and stare up at the mesmerizing view
of their
twinkle,
twinkle,
twinkle;
here and there,
flashing everywhere.
They'll coax you to happiness
no matter your amount of troubles.
So, fall into a starless sky of slumber.
But always remember their glow.
The stars,
amazing and beautiful.

Ten Paces and *Turn*

```
I ask you to holster the gun you
loaded with logic. Please, turn
   your           back.
   Give           me
   ten paces at
   least. Allow
   me a chance
   to best you
   with dreams.
```

Woodsy

The sun warms my skin.
The wind whips my hair.
I watch the water glisten,
eyes squinting against the glare.

There's a cozy crevice
where the rocks peak and dip.
When the sun and lake kiss,
only then will I quit.

The steady motion of the water repeats.
Birds come and go.
All from my makeshift seat,
I watch the whole show.

Soon, the wind is angry.
The trees sway in its rage.
Leaves fall like confetti
in celebration of the day.

I hate to think of leaving.
It comes with a certain burn.
But the creatures are all sleeping
and now, it is my turn.

Writing Minds

The world
occurs to me so
poetically it's smothering
I can't contain it all my mind
filled to the brim with words and
wants and whims if only I could swim
I must let the tide fall in waves of words
on beachy paper flow freely fail to waiver
give me a way to savor the secrets built into
my wall and just as I've emptied out something
turns on my mind's spout that I simply must
write about with just one rule above all: to
write my poetry in purple pen because I'll
look back on "way back when" and see the
mistakes I made then enduring in my
violet scrawl time capsules of emotion
drops of water in an ocean proof of my
every notion and I couldn't help but
write them all to writing minds
it's inescapable but of all
things to be capable
I am glad to be
unchangeable

Worse fates could always fall

Life is Poetry is Life

Life is but a poem,
short and simple
unless the poet
makes it long
and fantastic,
loud, colorful,
and dramatic.

The page is blank.
Sit and write.
Stay up all night if you must
to find and make your fate.
Don't wait.

When the page is full,
how will your poem end?

Thoughts, Judgment, and Lucidity

A thought occurred to me
concerning the lucidity
in which my thoughts occur.
Could my judgments possibly
not be what they were
in my earliest of years,
those in which all appears
in an air of simplicity,
an air that surely clears
in the presence of maturity?

And could it be the truth
that those well in their youth
thrive in untouched minds
and indulge in a sweet tooth
for new discoveries and finds?
Yet, when they pass from new to old,
just as their thoughts become too bold,
their minds—as sand to precious pearl—
are shaped into an ancient mold
and sent to understand the world.

And the way they once perceived
is left behind and unbelieved,
written off as imagination,
only to be, again, achieved
in elderly mental degradation:
the rise and fall of every peak.
And for those whose minds are unique,
could their thoughts, years ahead,
be heard as truth their thinker speaks
and valued before that thinker's dead?

*After*life at Sea

In a world where it's something else to wonder
and question what you see,
I stand alone on the shore
and question everything.

I wonder what the sky looks like
from the bottom of the sea.
And if lost sailors have a cemetery,
do the bodies of the drowned
help the coral grow?
Do the waves save only the worthy,
or do the souls of those that they don't save
stay with them eternally?

Imagine if they ride the tides
to anyplace they wish to be.
And the water swells with gossip
of every face they used to know.
And they make their homes in hidden caves
where no one living gets to go.
And they explore the world below our feet,
discovering hues we've yet to see
and music that is only made
when the deepest contours of the ocean floor
tremble and release their grief
and it rises to the surface
in an unheard harmony
so that the souls, eternally,
may have music with which to sing.
And if all this could be true,
is to die such an awful thing?

Half-Hopes

I have half a hope
that everything will work out.
But I don't expect
relief from this doubt.

I have half a hope
that my son will believe he was born from love.
But I don't expect
him to be any less confused than I was.

I have half a hope
that one day, I will need you and it will be my turn to.
But I don't expect
anything from you.

I have half a hope
that my half-hopes will prevail.
But I don't expect
that they will.

Maybe I Should Start Charging Late Fees

I feel like a library.
My soul made of pages,
hiding between covers,
compartmentalized,
alphabetized,
empty spaces left
for loaned-out pieces—

pieces of me
which accrue
a waiting list:
my time
and energy,
my patience
and compassion,
my open ears
and arms—
always switching hands,
but never landing home—

pieces of me
which I owe
to others:
my strength
and bravery,
my confidence
and drive,
the kind of love that comes
from an unbroken heart—
items I have specially ordered,
still flying in from far away—

pieces of me
which are
long overdue:
my sympathy
for myself,
my hope
for my future,
the kind of calm, clear mind
that maybe I never truly had—
these are the unreturned things,
for which maybe I should start to fee.

The Curse of Caring

It's just a burden, really,
to hold the heaviness of hope,
to have two eyes that can see
things of wonder in the wicked,
and to have a mind to know
that the world is deeply sickened.
But still a heart to love it so
and hands to hold a cure.
There's a way it can be fixed and
although it's failed before,
through and through the earth is sifted
and a seed is upward-staring.
Of this, I swear, I'm sure.
But I can see that doubt is glaring
from those I'm fighting for.
Disbelief is quite a force.
Its power, overbearing.
Maybe my cure is but a curse.
It is—the curse of caring.

A Typewriter Reality

Red lips love white smoke
and black lungs do too
like closing throats love to choke
on things they've never said
and little demons love to
dance within my head
like thin hands love to embrace
the chill of vacant space

Dark rooms love to be filled
and so do empty beds
like bottled thoughts love to be spilled
then wish to be unlearned
and every bridge we ever built
is begging to be burned
like you beg Him every night
to forgive your every sin

Dry tongues love to be drowned
and her sorrows do as well
like shaken girls savor the sound
of "I love you 'til the end"
and one silly little Christian
relentlessly pretends
that she didn't waste her youth
ignoring this one truth:

Our minds have all gone feeble
and our hearts have gone away
we're all paper people
in a typewriter reality
our words are everlasting
but we suffer from mortality
and we will always wear
the thoughts they couldn't bear to keep inside

An Old Mantra

I am the ugly friend.
That empty feeling is satisfaction,
contentedness.
Resistance is key.
Thin is pretty.
I am the ugly friend.

The Sad Child's Sacrifice

There's a sadness in my soul
and I'm afraid that I'm infectious.
So, please, don't come too close
for my breath, I'll have to hold
and I'll hold it my whole life
so you'll never catch this cold.

Fight or Flight *or Freeze*

Fight
Or
Flight

Or
Freeze

Sometimes
Swing
Or
Sprint
It doesn't matter

Sometimes
It serves you best
To choose the latter

With Water

Please don't tap
on my glass

the soul inside
spooks easily

the pain within
will spill and
fill all our lungs
with water

Imperfect Porcelain

A porcelain doll laden in lace,
a great loving heart, a lying face.
Brought up proper in the name of His power,
she now understands why He never found her
in confession with fingers crossed,
blaming Him for loved ones lost.
Living in a world with a stolen sun,
her perfect pink ribbon frayed and undone,
she walks with runs in her tights,
yells with tears in her eyes,
and falls to first-time lows
because after all, she knows:
God is the hope we hold
although he's callous, cold,
and ripped from our hands.
He is broken dreams and deserted plans.
Abandoned, abused, and led by a ruse
in the dimension of dementia
for the hair-brained and bruised,
we're made to believe no one's on their own
while destiny deems us, ultimately, alone.

Peace of Mind Hides in
The Acceptance of Our Sorrows

The room holds a certain air of history.
Rich with old things in broken boxes
and faded pictures on the mantelpiece,
with a bed that sinks on one side
and a floor that's always cold.
It chills his pale, wrinkled toes
as he climbs out of his sleep
and it creaks beneath his weight
as he shuffles toward the door.
He grabs his once-black hat
and lights his last cigar.
He turns the doorknob with a sigh
and as he steps outside into the world,
he feels the sun so rudely intrude
on the peace of a most quiet night.
It's evil, blinding, off-sprung rays
explore the contours of his aged face,
shining in attempts to melt away
the staleness of a life's dried tears.
But the man, he tips his old, worn hat,
tips it just in time
to stop all that light
from stealing all his sorrows.
He holds so dear to all his sadness,
all his despondency and grief,
and if begged to finally let it go,
he'd ask, "But why should I?
My aching heart doesn't hurt me
if I just let it breathe.
Let me ask you, young one,
what does one have to cling to
if not his tortured thoughts,
those through which
he proves himself alive?"
Then he'd stare into the stillness,
with his lungs both duly warmed,
his cigar now but a nub,
and he'd crawl back to his empty bed.

Red Lenses

It's been so long since I've seen something that wasn't
washed over in red. These colored glasses
have become such a part of me I thought the tops
of my ears and the bridge of my nose might actually miss them
if I ever set them on the nightstand. I've forgotten the
hues and shades, the tones and tints I used to marvel at before
my red lenses cast this light which creeps into every corner
keeping the darkness from the night. I worry about the way
my eyes might adjust to the searing burn of brightness and the
ways my brain might punish me for being so bold as to let the red
diffuse and begin to form the shapes of other colors, to remember
how beautifully they dance when they're allowed to be. But
today, I tipped my glasses just a touch, enough to judge
if the sun was still so piercing and the world so
    overwhelming,   and they were.

But I didn't squint.

Hell Is

Hell is where your dirty plans cross paths
Hell is the hole you hid me in
I am the hole you hid me in

Hell is breathing what isn't air
Hell is drowning in your eyes
I almost lost to you

Hell is living on your knees
Hell is in the high ground
I am on the high ground

Hell is where your home is
Hell has settled on your heart
I have not a fraction of a feeling

Hell is where we met
Hell is where we matched
I did nothing but burn

Hell is not wanting hope
Hell is in empty hands
I am in *Someone's* plans

Over The Years

Over the years,
I taught myself
to cry silently.

Over the years,
I taught myself
to smile differently.

Over the years,
I taught myself
to let the world change me.

Never again.

In Memory of Skyla Alves

You hear it happens everywhere,
that many have met the same fate,
it is becoming much less rare,
that the doctors were just too late.

We want to believe that terrible things
only happen *Elsewhere*,
that we will be spared from grief,
that life is fair.

Some rely on prayer,
some renounce faith
when they finally stare
the truth in the face.

But when tragedy hits home,
we become suddenly aware
that we are not alone.
We stand between us and despair.

Enough

The question is simple.
The answer, equally so.
And yet, still we ask ourselves,
as if we don't know,
"Could we ever
love fully,
laugh loudly,
give freely,
live proudly,
and fight bravely
enough
to keep your legacy alive?"
The answer: we must.

Lessons

I didn't go to college because of the debt I would have incurred.
But the lessons I've learned from this life
have cost me so much more than money.

Regrets

The risks
that make
regrets
are how
we learn
the world.

Unrecovered

I can't go back and
pretend I still have
the kind of hope that
hasn't yet been lost.

Choosing

The struggle of trouble
choosing an ending
is a phenomenon
reserved for
the literary life.

My First Performance

A dense crowd,
dimly lit.
The sting of tequila
on my tongue.
To sit,
and watch,
and wait
wouldn't be such torture
if not for the talking.
More than muted chatter.
Full conversations
cover the comedian,
the dancer,
even the band
in vocal clutter.

I am steady,
ready,
steeled against
the speaking.
I will be loud.
I will stand tall.
I will be proud.
I take the stage,
begin to read,
and suddenly,
silence—
enough to echo.
"Strange,"
I think.
But I continue to be
loud,
tall,
and proud.

And then,
the applause.

Amazing and beautiful.

LOVE

To wonder about love
To love for the first time
To love against reason
To lose love
To renounce love
To be found by love

The Treasured Queen

A twisting tale of a treasured queen,
of the first time her eyes held light,
the first time her heart would pine,
and the last time her heart would break,
of how she loved to brave the night
but fell victim to a shrine.

We begin, though, with a man unseen
and a most fortuitous mistake.
The moon hung hoarily above the land,
bent its neck to kiss the castle's peak,
embraced the glistening water of the lake
with the tender touch of a lover's hand.

The dust it left on tops of trees
soon fell upon her princess cheek.
He crept from home at that same hour,
seeking solace in the forest,
a place most utterly gaunt and bleak,
that Death itself would deem it dour.

He'd seen her often in his dreams,
never dared to think she could exist.
For each time the sun rose was his darkest day.
Afflicted by Misfortune's touch;
where he fled, it would persist
and any hope it scared away.

His life loose at the seams,
quantified, wouldn't merit much.
But she had the heaviest of hands.
Neither knew this of the other.
There they stood, in the underbrush,
a boy and girl from different lands.

And lost beneath a sky of leaves,
they hid beneath the most perfect cover.
When their eyes took their first look,
all surroundings became sparse
and, fading, left just one another,
meeting by a winding brook.

When stepping out into moonbeams,
God glanced upon their glowing hearts
and feeling that He mustn't tarry,
called His angels, "Sing thy song,"
to grace them both with His mark
so their hearts would match long after they're buried.

But as is the fate of treasured queens,
her love would not last forever-long,
was doomed that day to see an end
for Fate's eye knows not to blink.
Where one wanders, her gaze will wend.
A tale written in blood, not ink:

What is Love?

Is love
a light head,
a feverish blush,
a knotted stomach?
It sounds more like an illness.

Is it
anxiously waiting,
a constant need,
a recurring thought?
It sounds more like a disorder.

Is it
a gorgeous gown,
a true love's kiss,
happily ever after?
It sounds more like a fairytale.

Could I be a sick, unstable princess?

A Rose

Why is it, do you suppose,
that the mark of love
remains a rose?
A flower sees
a single fate:
to soil a vase and
be cast away. For what
reason would it not be a
fugitive of mortality which
a lover's instinct feels is due
when his life warrants worries
few? And when night brings sleep's
love display, but dreams fail to
transcend the truth of day,
it is more fitting for her
heart's key to be forged
of constancy, a symbol of
his stubborn hue that
should be awarded
to a wise girl who
better knows, who
never will accept
a rose.

Lost Constellations

You're a shooting star across my night sky.
Oh, how I love to watch you fly!
Yet, as I stare at where you are,
I realize it's not fair how far.
But the rise of the moon is
something I can share with you.
So, I wonder, are you staring too?

Picking Petals

Don't young girls grow in flowerbeds?
And don't they start as simple seeds?
And don't they, once they've been wed,
wither up to shrubs and weeds?

They live their lives in loveliness.
Yet, still longing to be plucked,
then give in to dreamlessness.
Oh, that I should have such luck!

I do away with what they want
because I've seen what comes of those
who try to love when they cannot.
Sad girls never really grow

for they pick petals of their own stems
while they're waiting to be sought
and, as they pick, they ask of them
if a man will love them or not.

If I should ever pick my petals,
each will be for a thing I've wished
and at the end, I'll tell myself
that I've been rightfully punished

because I know of, afterwards,
what these sacrifices bring
and they don't see that none endures
until they're left with nothing.

"This" *and* "That"

There's no need for me to list
every single "this"
that I could be for you.

I wouldn't ask you to combat
with every single "that"
that you could be for me.

I simply need to say
that, in every single way,
I could be your complement.

The Musician *and* The Poet

The musician
Plucks the strings of his guitar
The musician
Hums alone at a bar
The musician
Wishes in his melodies
For things he's seen in his dreams

The poet
Is squinting in a dark room
The poet
Scribbles sweet nothings and for whom?
The poet
Writes of love umpteen times over
In fear that no one will ever show her

The musician
Strums away, aware of the eye he catches
The poet
Writes of when gasoline first met matches

You've got the music
I've got the magic words
Let our song be one like the world has never heard

LOVE BOMB!

        We
        sat
         outside
           on
    the porch. He
picked up a cigarette.
We were talking. He
flicked the unlit cigarette
over the ash tray. He did
it a couple times before
he held a lighter
to the end of it. Each
time, I hid my smile so
he wouldn't notice
and stop.

No One's Watching

Thick smoke fills my throat
I let it escape my lips
Inhale it back into myself
Like I would the scent of you
A ghost
That's what I am
Or what I was
Some days I still feel myself fading away
The full moon is so symbolic
But I love Her when She's just a sliver
Hiding Her whole to see
Who will still love Her
When She's small
The fish must be sleeping on the pond's floor
Because the water doesn't breathe like I do
When you touch me
I press against your lips
Exhale smoke and love
Into your lungs
You remind me that I said
I hate public affection
And I say,
"No one's watching."

Eyes In the Sun

    I climb the same staircase
        Every night in all my dreams
            I climb the same staircase
                Into morning into Spring
            Feel the Summer heat at its peak
        And then I Fall down the stairs
    Into cold Winter snow
And as I climb again I know
    All its bends
        And where it winds
            An endless spiral
        In mundane time
    But now my foot
Has seemed to slip
    And where I land
        I cannot step
           So I race to outrun
        All the nothing I have done
    I flee from gravity
Because I've found
    Eyes in the sun
        And Luck and God—if you can hear—
            Let his sweet love endure
        His heart beats against my ear
and I can feel the future

What Hearts Are Meant For

It was so quickly that we reached the precipice,
the borderline,
edge of the cliff—
just shy of excellence.
Let the feeling caress you.
Close your eyes and let it possess you.
Save your grace and let it race—
that's what hearts are meant for.

Broad Silhouettes

Broad
silhouettes
roll through the
sky. They tell me
we are small.
The highest window's
breezy sigh compares
not to the mountain's
shortest wall. Trees like
peach fuzz on the mountain's
chin, a harrowing perspective.
Hike trails reveal its trodden
skin, ever something left to give.
A man-made gash runs down its side,
throbbing with a certain power—that of
human pride, which turns sweet to sour.
Rain-weighted clouds engulf its peak and to
the white, the sight is lost. Suddenly, it
seems so meek, that such a flimsy foe, it cannot
cross. Here, I sit, thoroughly enthralled, with
the one who makes me brave. As we stare out at the
mountain's monstrous sprawl, we feel small, but safe.

Entirely, *Eternally*

If the world
should freeze over
entirely
I would hope to be
encapsulated at your side
eternally

Our First Home

I hate this apartment
Small and cramped and narrow
I hate the way the roof leaks
And the tub clogs
I hate the way the kitchen floor slants
And the coarse carpet in the living room
I hate the way the electrical outlets
Are too loose to hold a plug
And especially the dead mice
The cats leave at our door
But of all the things I hate about this apartment
There is something I love more

It's our first home

More of *YOU*

I have wanted more
        And more
     And more
Of you
Since the moment we met

I wished to feel your breath
            Your touch
       Your kiss
And you
When I hadn't had you yet

And having had your gripping
          Consuming
     Paramount
Love
As we kiss through blended sweat

I still want more
        And more
     And more
Of you
Every chance that I get

The *Sweetest* of Dreams

Every morning my eyes open
knowing they will see you.
Still, every time we say "goodbye,"
I hate that we have to.

In the first moment
my heart feels a distance
between it and yours,
mine's already missed it.

I crave the sound of your voice
and your hanging laughter in the air
in every second of silence
and every word I share.

When you hurry home to me
or I to you,
I'm sure that we must be
the subject of Luck's pursuit.

I savor the warmth of your arms
and the feel of your kiss,
wishing that time could go on,
suspended just like this.

And as I lay by your side,
as selfish as it seems,
I hope to see you again
in the sweetest of dreams.

When The Stars Lived With Us

When the first moonflower blooms
and the world settles down to sleep,
when the first nightingale croons
for a lover he can keep,
long locks like starless night
fall in an unruly mane
and she emerges from a petal bed of white
in a gown made of the same.

She stretches her long limbs
and rubs stardust from her eyes.
She tiptoes on the flower's brim
and then, begins to fly!
She takes her throne
and looks out into the endless space.
She remembers how the Earth has grown,
caresses its grateful face.

The glowing goddess of the night
prances blindly as she's pining.
She needs no mirror nor omniscient eye
to know that she is shining.
She lights the Earth with love
to the crickets' high-pitched drum
and lured by this, down from above,
curious constellations come.

They gleam in admiration of her,
helping to relieve the world's weight
and as they grow to love her,
She will a million times reciprocate.
But one dark night, you and I,
wrapped warmly up together
caught a lone wandering eye
and a star fell from its tether.

It came to live with us,
forging a new route,
drawn by our love and trust,
and the rest soon followed suit.
We hoarded them within our home
and ensured they were content,
in fear of being left alone
in the dim light of the crescent.

But one star had stood by the moon
and he was loyal to her still.
At the risk of her heart breaking soon,
he performed her every will.
He cast a fishing rod down to the world,
reeled every roof off every wall,
and when he found where they were,
we learned, still loyal were they all.

They missed her unmatched grace,
longed for her inviting smile.
We each have one rightful place
and they'd known theirs all the while.
They rose, happy to ascend,
toward the one, as we all must,
to which their gaze will always wend.

But we will always remember when the stars lived with us.

ALL the Little Things

They always said it was
all the little things
that make life worth living—
from each small moment
which string into a memory,
to each choice we make,
slowly deciding who we will be.
I was told they all hold value.
I've found this difficult to believe.

I always thought it was
all the little things
that ruined larger entities—
from a suddenly raised voice
and the things no one thinks a child sees,
to each harmful quip
and the insecure soul it appeased.
I have felt the little things
cast a shadow over me.

So, when it turned out to be
all the little things
that led to the moment we met—
from a small town
and the boredom it begets,
to your untroubled smile
and the soul it befits—
I began to see the value
in little things, I must admit.

And now that it has come to be
all the little things
that had me make an unsafe bet—
from an uninhibited laugh
and the flick of an unlit cigarette,
to a wink across a crowded room
and a gaze that whispers the word "yet."
I am grateful for all the little things
that changed my mind when it was set.

Sunken Footsteps

A love that rides the rocking waves,
is colorful and bright.
When the sun rises from the haze,
we reflect the light.

We are made of different hues.
I, deep navy.
You, shimmering aquamarine.
I am made of midnight blues
and you are sea foam green.

We mix and fade and change
beneath a seemingly calm surface,
and when the tide rolls away,
this does not deter us.

The ocean mist gently rests on our cheeks
and all our sunken footsteps
stretch far across the beach.
We watch the water as it ebbs.

It will come flooding back
suddenly and swiftly,
announced by a thunder crack
when the wind is feeling shifty.

Waves will crash against the shore
and the call of the collision
will leave lookers-on wanting more
of such a gripping vision.

From Smoke to Water

From my fishbowl, I can see two eyes
staring back at me. They're filled with
smoke, thick and gray, and what they
hold can't be explained. My heart
beats each time they blink. As they turn from
smoke to water, I see in them an altar and a father.
I see small newborn faces. I hear my heart breaking record
paces as they stare up at me with those same eyes that have
guaranteed that I will never have to be alone—a certainty I'd
never known until I felt what it is to be found, and the world
turned topside-down and all the inches I had shrunk—and all
that way that I had sunk—suddenly, I stood and grew—suddenly,
I turned and flew! You saw me so differently, as someone I
still hope to be. But everything looks beautiful when viewed
through a beautiful lens. So, in those smoke-filled eyes I
must devote every last ounce of my trust and hope that when
they turn to water, they will not stray an inch farther—
hope that each and every day, they may see me
the same way—hope that they may always
be just a glance away from me.

The Suppliant

Dear Love, please, promise me
you'll resemble not the winged liberty
of those creatures who are most sought,
whose heart and whims differ not,
who stray at signs of new delight,
and who forfeit not a chance for flight.

Dear Birds, in all your vanity,
tell not my love to flee from me
as you may from sights you've seen
to those which you have never been
because whatever feels most new
receives your love and all of you.

And Love — oh please! — do not reply
with the plight of those who cannot fly,
who flaunt their feathers' vibrant shades
and dance about in their best way
to gain the sole attention of
one who will not give her love

because her long, one-spotted feathers
make her feel as though she is better
than anyone whose eye she's caught
or anyone who's ever thought
that she was more, 'til — truth befall! —
peacocks are the most superficial of us all.

All that I can ask of you
is that you, Love, long overdue,
not leave my life 'til it is gone
and meet us in our second dawn.
See us through our every day
and, to you, I may begin to pray.

Between Us

Between us,

there is a lie afoot.
I don't know
who or what it is.
But it's there,
somewhere

between us.

Watch the Sky

I'm afraid.
I need him now.
I don't know what I'll do
if I break again.
Tonight, we sat outside
in the storm
and watched the sky.
When lightning struck,
electric violet veins
pulsed through the clouds,
and I longed to feel that powerful.

The Third Moon

If one moon may satisfy a world,
why, then, might some see three?
And to the night's lonely queen,
what pleasure could a kingdom be
when, to her sky, she may only cling
until the sun unveils its spiteful face
and, ascending all those ancient stairs,
settles into her rightful place?
Then, weighed back down by all she bears,
The moon again awaits her time.
And when the sun's tired neck has bent,
the moon again begins to climb
and in her sky, finds her complement:
a sight to which she'd formerly been blind,
a life to which she could not compare,
a beauty of her own kind
wrapped in grace she could never wear.
And in her pining, she will miss
the lurking presence of another,
a third moon in her palace
who will soon become her lover's lover.
But not before she's won his heart
and not before he holds her own.
Not then, but after their love's start,
the third's intentions will be known.
And as his orbit changes center,
and his love is re-devoted,
into new galaxies she'll venture,
his choices duly noted.
She will ask herself: is it worse
to drift through space, solitary,
or to suffer heartbreak's curse
as the third moon of three?

A Covetous Heart

There once was a boy born unto the sky
to whom earthly rules failed to apply.
A covetous heart lured him down.
Yet, among the clouds still rests his crown.
Now, there endures in him a wish to fly
in spite of the fact that he must comply
to the laws and limits of the ground.
In his youth, he often dreamt of flight
and although he tried with all his might,
and had his journey long since planned,
he learned upon reaching his desperate hand
high into the unforgiving night
in attempts to its deepest pits, alight,
that Fate carries not who it befits to stand.

All Your Hearts

You
built
your house
of playing cards,
tried to make it home,
took your seat on the ace
of spades, dictated from your
throne, held all your hearts at
ransom, piled diamonds on the floor,
you clubbed me with your love, somehow
left me wanting more. I didn't dare breathe
for we could topple with a touch. But you lost
what held real value for not treating it as such.

My Love

It took so long to make this mask
So I could wear it and fool everyone
I worked so hard to fake this laugh
At all that can't be undone
I heard whispers of your lies
I watched you look away
A novel in your eyes
You couldn't make them stay
Now you're trying not to think of me
Not to see me in her place
Well, my love, I hope I'm on your mind

You said such beautiful things
Now I bet she hears the same
But wouldn't it be funny
If you called her by my name?
Wouldn't it be funny?
It'd be the day you called and I never came
The day you realize you miss me
And that things will never be the same
Now you're trying not to think of me
Not to see me in her place
Well, my love, I think I'm on your mind

Why do you keep switching sides?
I swear I'll push you off this fence
Why do you keep looking behind?
This wood wasn't made to bend
You swear you're on one side
I'll throw stones 'til you've fallen to one end
Make up that mind
You'll never fall again
Now you're trying not to think of me
Not to see me in her place
Well, my love, I know I'm on your mind

The Secret of the Sea

Dark waves and moonlight kisses
embrace in forbidden feels
and pine for stolen glances
as water trickles
          u
          p
          w
    a
        r
  d,

licking friendly fog.
The murky reflection of a supernova
reveals the secret of the sea
and carried away in the claws
of a great fleeting fowl,
it hides among lost constellations
and rides a tortured melody.
And come dawn, come sun-soaked day,
vices sprout as newborn roses
from the palm of an open hand
and crawling down to the crook of the arm,
revel in flawed perfection.

An Ode to Those Loved Only in Their Dreams

The Sleeper awakens,
blindly seizing the remnants of a dream.
With reaching arms and clawing fingers,
she clings to a blissful slumber,
a world full of wantedness
where she lies on a grassy hill,
watches the clustering of clouds,
tastes the whispers of the wind,
hears the weeping of the willow.
A world where the birds still sing
and the sun still smiles
and so, she does the same,
humming along to a beautiful lullaby,
suspending herself in sleep.
A world where she is chased not by fright,
but by the fear of being unseen,
running solely to be sought
through her own limitless mind.
Her pursuer that of perfection,
he holds her in his hands
and wraps her in his heart.
She wallows in his warmth
for the loveless reality
brought by lackluster light:
the world where she is just one trifled figure
amongst a whole of broken homes and hearts,
where she has slipped like sand
through salted waves of fingers
not to be caught,
but slipping precisely
into the footsteps of the fallen.
Her pain is not unique but common even.
Her tears shed from the eyes of others
have marked the same skin-stained path,

tracing cheeks and crescent lips,
down the curves of chins.
The difference is the sting of loss
is so much greater when it strikes oneself.
It cuts the sky and lights the soul,
burning as a scorching sun
whose spherical followers
have fled from around it.
So, one question tickles her mind
and licks at her lips:
What was it worth to put such strain
into the feat of pulling gravity
to earn the love of just one floating orb,
to lose that one and push the rest away?

For what is it to be the center of nothing?

Close Your Eyes

A cheated woman is closer to a loaded gun
than any weapon man could make
and a broken woman's shaking hand
can be the best of shots,
will aim at he who held her close
enough to stop her breath
and set her sights on the life
of that gruesomely masked man.
Her hand will take just a second to make
the last decision he'll ever see
and the piece of metal that emerges,
more menacing than anything its size,
in the seeming several years
before it meets his skin,
will turn to tears, then seep into his chest.
Finally,
she will release the breath she had held
from the moment she chose to close his eyes
to that in which she realized
she couldn't watch them close.

I Thought with The Butterflies *and* It Was the Death of Me

I thought not with my head
nor even with my heart,
but with the butterflies I felt.
I followed on the whims they went,
away from things on which I dwelt.

I let them consume myself
'til I was made of precious wings
and after long, restless nights,
we collected our precious things
and took off in butterfly flights.

Such fickle little creatures
who love for only moments
before they change their minds
because they know that, in this world,
there are always lovelier things to find.

But even they favor a flower,
one of the most becoming kind.
And they led me where they wished,
back to this favorite flower,
in the love for which I perished.

Beneath the Sea

I am a tidal wave.
You won't notice me retreating
beneath the ocean's surface.
You won't feel the speed I'm gaining
against its craggy floor.
You won't even know I'm gone
until I am halfway around the world.
But you will feel my absence
in the first moment you wet your toes
and in the waves that lap at your feet,
in the way the water rocks you around
and in the swells that sing you to sleep.
I will make it an entire world away.
But we both know
once I round the bend,
I can only come back.
All the momentum I have built
will have me barreling back to you.
And we also know once I arrive,
I can only crash.
I'm sorry for the carnage I make.
I'm sorry for the irreparable break.
I'm sorry I always leave you in my wake,
wishing I was back beneath the sea.

The Mirror

I
wonder
which of the
one-more-chances
broke your heart.
Maybe it was each one.
If a heart shatters in
a broken home, does it make
a sound? Maybe I just didn't
hear it falling over and over
again. Or maybe the first time was
like a pebble against a windshield.
Maybe it was watching the crack spread
that tore me apart. One phantom half of
me sweeps pieces of you into a pile. The
other side gets a running start, diving
into the bed of jagged edges as if they
were freshly fallen leaves. I want to
hurt in the same places I hurt you.
I want to bleed for you. I want to
relieve you of the burden you've
carried since I handed you my
heavy heart. I know you want
those things too. Take
comfort in the fact
that my heart
broke along
with yours,
as if I was
the
mirror
you
stood
before,
every
single
time.

The Princess Who Loves the Peasant

The princess who loves the peasant
puts her jewels in a drawer,
pulls a hood over her hair,
walks among her worshippers.

The princess who loves the peasant
wants for naught but nothing,
the quietness that brings clarity,
the darkness that breeds light.

The princess who loves the peasant
is doomed to continue
to devalue and diminish
until she disappears.

Ninety Percent

When I say you are
ninety percent skull,
you hear,
"ten percent brain."
But I never said
that your head
was the whole of you.
Of every inch,
and ounce,
and atom,
ninety percent
is made of thick,
impermeable marrow,
deep and dense.

Should Be

I've heard you say
a thousand times,
"That's not how it
should be."
As if you decide
how the world
should be.
As if you decide
how I
should be.
And as long
as you try to,
neither will stop
disappointing you.

Woman vs. *Wind*

A woman screamed into the wind.
She told it her hopes,
dreams,
fears,
desires.
She told it she wanted
to be learned before loved.
She told it she wanted
to raise a man
no woman would ever fear.
She told it she wanted
her words to sweep the world
and change the way it sees
through certain eyes,
even in some small way.

"Why don't you understand?"
She asked the wind,
pushing against it with all her power,
walking sideways through the world.
"I've given you everything:
All of my words
and all of my will.
When will you allow me a reprieve,
find me in my grief,
offer sweet relief
from the dizziness?"

Finally, the wind subsided
and it replied with,
"I can't hear you
over the sound of myself."

To Beg

You didn't hear me.
So, I asked you to listen.
But you didn't hear.
So, I asked again.
I asked,
and I asked,
and I pleaded.
Until finally,
I asked you to hold my pride
while I begged.

And you heard me.
But you didn't understand.
So, I explained.
And when it didn't sink in,
I tried again.
I dug deeper within myself
so I could clarify,
and give context,
and add afterthoughts.
Until finally,
I asked you to hold my dignity
while I begged.

And now, you understand.
But I'm underwhelmed
and unarmed
for the next phase of battle.
I have neither my pride
nor my dignity
with which to beg you
to care.

In The Landing

You've taken every one of the difficult things
you've faced and buried them deep underground,
constantly adding to your anti-treasure trove.
And when I came to you with my difficult things,
holding them under the sun for you to see,
you buried them along with yours.
And each time I pulled them out,
you put them back.

I wanted you to turn them
into true treasure.
Glue them,
sand them,
paint them,
display them on a shelf.
But I should have noticed from the start
that you didn't do that with your own.
I should have noticed when I felt
my feet leave the floor
and in the wind on my face
as you carried me
to your hole in the dirt.
And if not in the fall,
I finally noticed in the landing.

In So Many Words

I've said the same thing
in so many words.
So many different words.
But you didn't hear it.
And then,
you didn't hear it.
And again,
you didn't hear it.
I told you who I am,
what I want,
and what I need.
But as I spoke,
you only thought
of ways to correct me.
You should have taken me
at my word—
words—
so many words.
You think you know
my heart better than I do
because you've held it
for years.
And you may have,
by now,
had you taken the time
to turn it over in your hands,
to study all its sides.
But you never learned to love
the parts of me you didn't like
and I bear the guilt of not changing
each time I must fight for
what I have already pled for
in so many words;
a fight fueled by stubbornness,
not strength,
because I cannot change
and I will not go on
punishing myself
for not being what you
believe me to be.
Maybe one day,
you'll come to see
the ringing in your ears
is the truth
of my many words.

Multiple Choices

The choices are:
    A. Understood
    B. Fulfilled
    C. None of the above

You failed the test
And I lost my love

You'll step into something new
When you've outworn them
I almost wish
Someone would warn them

You'll say it wasn't as bad
As I say it was
And they'll never know
What you stole:
Everything I had

*In*secure

What if I said
that everything
anyone ever said
about me,
especially you,
was true?
Then,
would you be happy?
If I called
every insult
a fact,
would that bring
a smile to your face?
Would that put me
in my place?
Would you be satisfied?
If you said I was selfish
and I agreed;
if you said I was stupid
and I said I was sorry;
if you said I was ugly
and I said I knew;
if you said I was useless
and I said it was true,
then,
would you feel better about yourself?

With*out* Me

Those twisted lies you told me
Have never been spoken so honestly
You fooled me with falsity
Well, good luck 'cause
Now you're fucked without me

I stopped my life to save yours
From yourself
I put my own dreams on
The bottom shelf
Anyone close to me
Became my enemy
When they tried to deny
My first real chance to fly
Turns out I was the blind one
You don't want a perfect woman
I hope you find one
Who treats you worse than I can

No one is ever truly ready
Even if they are
they hold their scars too close to be free
I thought you could let your burdens be
But good luck 'cause
Now you're fucked without me

Well, there goes those years I wasted
That's all my fears I faced them
Those sacred wings you gave me
You ripped from my back so suddenly
I didn't know I was falling
Until the ground came calling
And when I landed flat on my face
I took a good look around
You'd vanished without a trace
And I was nowhere to be found

What a shame I couldn't see
That you held those goddamn scars
too close to be free
But how blind could you be
Not to see that you'd be
Fucked without me?
Well, good luck 'cause
Now you're fucked without me

Mortar Seals

The way you lay there
After I asked you to leave
The way you lay there
With only yourself to please
You don't seem to comprehend
The words I use to say
That I am no longer your home
You want to blame someone
I know you blame me
You want to hate someone
You know I hate me
I carried the bricks
That built your insecurity
I've pounded my fists
On the wall
With all of my will,
But I took time
With each mortar seal
I filled
And it's always harder
To fix
Than to build

The Thirst

You break my heart
On your way in
And again
On your way out
And you never even
Look back
When you leave

When you leave
The dawn to turn
My home to dust
When you leave
The daylight
Looking for you
And the afternoon,
Evening,
And night
Spent losing you
Amongst the clouds
Searching the sky for
A sign of you

A sign of you
Sometimes I put on my ring
And pretend it isn't
The only unbroken thing
Between us
That it won't outlast us
Sometimes I pretend
That you would take on
Monsters for me
That you would fight
Gallantly
That you would set
The world on fire
For my sake

For my sake
I won't have
The hand of reality
Anywhere near my cheek
It will sting,
And burn,
And bruise
In a way which
I fear feeling
In a way from which
I'm unsure I can recover
In a way from which
I'm certain
I cannot

I cannot
Fathom how you do it
Come and go
Leave a trail of crumbs
You know I won't follow
Spout a fountain of words
That are dazzlingly hollow
Clearly, I thirst
For dizzying sorrow

Days Sober

Maybe I'm an addict,
waking each morning to tally the day,
always moving towards the moments
that make me start over.
Maybe somewhere down the line,
I learned to love the way
the sunlight sears my brain
and my muscles move a little slower,
the vertigo, dark spots,
the way the colors fade,
and every vicious noise
that echoes through the hangover.
All I know is when it comes to you,
there's only one thing I can say,
I've survived,
____ days sober.

His Frozen Throne

He
likes to
walk in the
snow. Why he
does she'll never
know. She thinks he
must be awfully cold
when he sinks his feet
into the snow.

She wishes she could
keep him warm, but she
can't reach his ragged
form. So she sits and
sulks, forlorn, stuck in
the strangest kind of storm.

The kind where there's
no flakes that fall, no
frosted windows or icy
walls. On the ground,
there's snow, that's all.
But there's no frozen
flakes that fall.

There's just one man who
walks alone along a series
of white roads. Where
they lead, they never
show. He just sinks
knee-deep
in snow.

And
when she
tries to call
his name, the
words that left
and those that came
have changed and do
not sound the same,
were blown *a p a r t*
along their way.

She begs him, "Come
back to me, always stay
where I can see." He
hears "Why don't you
leave? Just go, you've
ruined everything!"

And that tricky wind that
broke those words blows
them onto separate worlds
and they fly like broken
birds, trying to reach him
on his world.

Sadly, he's a different
person now. He lives
the way the snow allows,
and as he's sinking
farther down, he
makes himself
a lonely
town.

And
he lives
there on his
own, sitting on
a frozen throne
deep within his
frozen home with
just one wish to be
left alone.

But sometimes she
thinks she sees air
rise from where he
breathes and she
shouts, "Come home
please!" but he's too
low to hear her pleas.

So, she intends to pull
him out and he refuses
to be found. But she'll
tunnel to the ground in
hopes to find what stays
unfound.

And just as their paths
will cross, she'll dig
deep into the frost,
down to the dirt
and moss, but
she'll be late
and he'll be
lost.

Blackened Bridges

Your sweatshirt smells like rain
Black drops on sleeves of gray
Clouded skies I notice as
I watch you drive away
Come back to me
Clouded eyes there's no disguise
I feel you drift away
Come back to me
The clouds all die I try to find
The days we wasted away
Where cut ties and blackened bridges spoon
They'll be falling asleep beneath the man in the moon

We Were Made with Two Hands
So We Could Hold Our Own When We're Alone

He serves as her drug,
but his drug is real.
She's addicted to his love,
but he's addicted to how it feels
to accept his illusions
and to have the power to erase
anything he pleases,
any hint or trace
of the scent of his sorrows
and the essence of his home.
"Just one more time," he says,
"And then I'll leave you alone."
But he puts his promise in a pile
with all his broken things
because he just hates sinking
and loves having wings.
Yet, every time he cries,
he tells himself, "One more time."
He says it again
as his fears walk down the line.

Meanwhile, she lies in bed
and waits for him to call.
She holds her own hand
and stores her worries in the wall.
She knows what he's been doing.
She couldn't make him stop.
She saw all his tears hit the floor.
She couldn't keep them from the drop.
And suddenly, she feels
that tonight will be the night
that her blindly swinging fists
will finally lose their fight.
As she feels him slip away,
out of his world of woe,
she looks to her wall of worries
and sees the words: "You let him go."

I Called to You from the Caveside and I Waited

We entered together,
enchanted with uncertainty
and unfazed by fear,
trading roles:
leader,
follower,
carrier,
carried.
We explored the contours
of the hidden earth
beneath our feet,
staring into the dark, the deep,
while the light behind grew dim.
Our hands, latched,
failed to detach
through so many falls.
We scraped through,
we scraped by.
Such a sweet,
scraping ascent;
a subtle form of torture.

But I slipped,
lost my grip,
and you were gone
so suddenly.
I waited for you
and I cried
and eventually,
I called to you
while I climbed
and when I made it
out, I waited.
Did you hear me calling,
as long and as loud as I could
to coax you out from within?

I watched that dim light
down the way
disappear.
I heard an echo.
It sounded like you
letting go.

I would have died
by that cave side
if you had only
let me.

When You Let Her Go

Long, golden locks
and cold, ivory skin
trapped inside a lonely box,
hiding from within.

You came with curious eyes,
looked and looked again.
But, much to your surprise,
she'd locked herself in.

You had always held the key,
as you would quickly realize,
and you so foolishly released
the key to your demise.

For when you let her go,
she began to see
there is no such thing as "no"
and nothing she can't be.

A *Love* Letter

Dear Love,

If I promise to hide, do you promise never to find me?

> Signed,
> *Me*

Don't Stop

Sometimes I still think of you
Sometimes it feels so good
I tell myself to stop
Sometimes not to

Hot Air Balloon Love

I've never been in
a hot air balloon—
I'm terrified of heights—
but I imagine it's a lot
like falling in love—
with which I am far
too familiar—the
gravity growing
beneath your
feet, the

certainty
that they
will feel
the ground
again soon.

Freer

I used to have wings,
back when I was on my own.
Back then, I could've flown.

But I ripped them from my back
without so much as a wince
and I haven't seen them since.

I've thought I had everything.
But time has told
and I have grown.

Though the scars burn
and I may never fly again,
I am freer now than I was then.

The Root
of All
Happiness

Every woman has the means
to capture either a man's heart
or his body.
Her happiness relies not
on which she acquires,
as that is destined to be what it will,
but on which she desires.

The Root of All *Unhappiness*

Unhappiness stems
neither from love
nor heartbreak,
but from having it
in one's nature
to care
transcendently more
for others
than anyone
will ever care
in return.

The Other Cheek

If, in your mind, they love you,
I won't touch you with the truth.
But when the setting sunlight fades from their face
and you start to feel the soft fingers of sorrow;
when the moon will soon take its place
and you wish for a never-tomorrow;
when reality has slapped,
I hope you turn the other cheek.

And Maybe the *First*

I remember
the tip of your finger
tracing my spine,
the shock
and the shiver;
the last time I felt
fueled passion
and desire,
and maybe the first;
the last time I felt
almost anything;
the last time I failed to feel
disgusted at a touch;
the last time I felt
a little bit of future,
and maybe the first.

A Lonely Bird

I
locked
my
heart
into a birdcage.
I threw the key over
my shoulder. She sings
all through the night.
But no one will ever
hold her. She's lived
so happily this way,
to be only seen and
heard—at least I
don't think she is
a lonely bird.

Poison Blood

Is a person
Without a purpose
Still considered such?
Is the poison blood
That pumps through
My haunted heart
Capable of being loved?

The Child

He found her on the hardwood
with her cheek pressed to the floor.
Her tears had all run their race,
her breaths had all but left her.
He hovered, then, above her,
gazing unto her frame,
and, folding in his ancient wings,
took to the ground beside her.
She met his eyes and shied away.
She knew what he would bring.
She did not wish to gain his aid.
He'd failed her once before.
But this small boy would attempt
to afflict her yet again.
He held his bow straight ahead
and the arrow seemed to say,
"I've come back for you, my dear.
My sweet, I have returned.
There's no need for fear this time.
I'm sure I've got it right."
She stared into its eye
as it aimed straight at her heart.
She looked to its beholder
and spoke her spiteful words,
"You're nothing but an infant,
a confused little thing!
How are you to know
with whom I am meant to be?"
He seemed unstartled by her thoughts
and, simply, he replied,
"I've lived a life of immortality
which you could never fathom.
There exist such horrid things
of which you couldn't dream.
I've seen, with my own eyes,
parents bury their children
and men take lives of strangers
in the name of the same god.
And you take your heart as broken
when you've suffered just one loss.
My dear, you know no pain but yours.
The child here is you."

Fitting

Somewhere, someone's
jagged broken
edges are
just begging
to meet
mine, aching
to align.
We will
know we
could only
have broken
for the
sake of
fitting into
one another.

Lunar Tears

I know your heart has grown heavy,
it'll take but a moment to fall.
You're missing a sense of sanctity.
Just know, my dear, it evades us all.

I know your days have no dawn
and all your light is masquerading.
I know your nights are ever-long
and lunar tears are cascading.

The skies, they weep on you alone,
and the passersby, they stare.
But I promise you not one will slow
to ask you how you fare.

They'll watch as the rain will pour
and they'll say they didn't see
all the tears that came before
the night you chose to leave.

You'd lived through too much pain
and you knew you couldn't bear
to live to see another day,
but you saw me standing there.

I gave you the love they borrowed
and all the courage that they stole
and you let me keep your sorrows
in a bottle of my own.

I took it away, planning to
drown it in the endless sea
because, just as it was hurting you,
it had begun to grow on me.

But, instead, I chose to remove the top
and see the things you used to see.
Then, I felt my own heart drop
And now, I wait for someone like me.

The Isle

Like an enraged wind
of the tempest she resides in,
she has blown all away.
Isolated, they lay in her wake,
sinking in the sea,
reborn from the sanded floor.

She stands alone—an isle.

Her shores are silent and still,
have been so for quite a while,
ever since they stopped arriving.
But one lonely sailor wanders aimlessly,
lost and disconcerted,
with no desire to escape.

The *Shadow* of a Doubt

I tell myself I hate to lie
But is it the same to hide?
You don't know who you're seeing
I don't know who I'm being
Choked are the words you're reading
Just like the breaths I'm breathing
When it runs away
Sew my shadow to my feet
So that when I nod my head
It doesn't disagree
Replace my shadow heart
Hold it 'til it starts to beat
Remind me that I can live without
Living as the shadow of a doubt

Hospice for Broken Hearts

My broken heart was beating slowly.
The doctors said I wouldn't love.
They told me to rest for the rest of my days—
or my lack thereof.

I did as they instructed.
I let my heart sleep soundly
and, just when I'd adjusted,
you found me.

You came, at first, to numb the pain
and bring light into the day
and soon, you had me foolishly
begging the sun to stay.

But, like the morning hours,
I was sure your light was fleeting
and yet, on nights I thought of you,
I noticed a noise—a beating.

It hastened at the sound of your voice.
It shook my entire chest.
My heart had finally awoken
from its long and dormant rest.

Now, I walk myself to the door.
The doctors watch in awe of me,
not quite sure what they did right,
applauding my recovery.

MORE LOVE

Your love:
it fills me up
until there's
more love
than hate
and suddenly,
and finally,
I'm free.

A Song

The clouds roll over the moon
and it's all that I can do
not to call you when I'm sad
The stars lean down at night
and whisper that I just might
call you one day when I'm happy
because something I couldn't do
is to burden you with me

But if I should ever leave this town
I know that I must be
ready to release my crown
as the queen of the lonely

For all it takes to rid myself
of my misery is to be
somewhere else
Happiness awaits me and
it's in your hands
All that I must do is to plan
the journey of a
lifetime spent with you

But if we should ever leave this town
I know that I must be
ready to release my crown
as the queen of the lonely

The clouds reveal the moon
and its light shines down on you
to tell me where I should be
The stars are burning bright
in hopes that I just might
thank them one day 'cause they
showed me to you

And now that I am here with you
it seems to me I just know
all that came before us has faded into
the burden I have let go

Because I will leave this town
and one day I will be
wearing a new crown
as the queen of the redeemed

What I Love Most About *You*

What I love most about you
is the way you seem to float.
My favorite feeling in the world
is the world leaving my toes.

What I love most about you
is that you want to watch me fly.
My favorite feeling is the way
we are untouchable in the sky.

What I love most about you
is that I will always know
I will never lose the feeling
that keeps me from fearing what's below.

The Birds' Window

Evening winds and the soft scent of pine
blow lightly in the drapes over my mind,
and carry with them undue flattery,
words of splendid beauty mine,
words that once made matter of me.
The nightingales still trill and croon
in hopes that I might give a second swoon.
Yet, burst their lungs, as seems to be their will,
I foresee that, come bright light of noon,
they will seek still darker rooms to fill
because the sun, in its effulgent pride,
then finds itself where I reside
and at its high, twelfth-hour peak,
I am blinded to its setting side
and each other hour is rendered weak.
Here, Noontime will never slow
for all Times will their turns forgo.
Here, the sun will forever shine
so that I may close the birds' window
and I, myself, may cease to pine.

Hints & Traces

There are always hints beforehand
Always traces left behind
Love is far from finite
And seldom self-confined

You'll see its headlight in the fog
You'll hear its faint but growing horn
Long before the train buzzes by
Long before love is born

It passes all too quickly
You can try to wave it down
But if you miss your moment
It won't come back around

As you watch it fade from view
As you wish and will it to come back
It will leave you savoring
The rattle in the track

True *and* Real

There's something I'm missing
It's a way to feel complete
Because some nights all I can think
Is that alone is such an awful way to sleep
I need organic warmth
A heat that could but wouldn't leave
I feel as though I'll fade away
Without two arms holding me

There's something I long for
That I fear I'll never feel
One day I hope Luck graces me
With a love that's true and real
I gave my heart once before
I saw no reason to conceal
But it was not returned to me
And now it isn't there to steal

There's something I've hid from
For quite a while now
I'd still like to think I long for love
But I'm not sure I would know how
And should I stare Love in the face
I'm not sure I would allow
Myself to feel the weight of it
It would just drag me down

There's something that has found me
After quite a search ensued
I held it off long as I could
And for that I apologize to you
You filled my heart with joy
Fear and apprehension too
But you proved to me
That I could be loved so real and so true

Gatsby's Green Light

A waterfall of
amethysts and emeralds
rushes out to a gemstone sea.
The turning tides
will toss and churn you.
They are most unkind.
As you fall to the ocean floor,
you may lose the light above.
The sand may strip
the glint from your surface.
But you were not made
to shine only with the sun,
to reflect its cheap trickery.
You are meant to be
some Gatsby's green light,
your emerald glow only visible
to a certain eye.

Wait, my dear.
Wait to be seen,
to be dived and dug for,
to be treated like treasure.
I beg you.

The Wordsmith

Deep within a wooded land,
there lives a wordsmith in his lair.
He once embraced the light of sun.
But now, without a window near,
is a fallen lover of the night.
A rumpled man in a wooden chair,
he stares at parchment white as snow
and a brick wall built up on fear
and, sullenly, he recollects,
runs a hand through salted hair,
slips himself through woolen sheets,
and tries to make the clouded clear.
A faded thought of a fateful day
when he first saw her standing there.
Her step was light, her eyes alive,
her hand in that of a man, austere.
But he was young and braver then,
had never seen someone so fair,
and God forbid he let her leave,
he'd stay, and she'd not reappear.
He'd have spent his life bound by regret,
wishing to receive a spare,
wondering how much time truly passes
within the passing of a year.
Pity he who cannot recall
the life they filled with love so rare;
the first time when, in our world,
not one eye shed a single tear.
His feeble mind remembers naught
of the simple grace she used to wear
or their exchange to end all infamy
on the rooftop of the Belvedere.
The utterings of his silver tongue
dissolved into thick, mystic air
and just before the wind blustered by,

were heeded by her gilded ear.
One, but they, is yet to see
the secret dance their words shared.
They took a bow and the curtain fell
too soon for one to overhear.
But legend goes that they paused,
for a stranded second in midair,
were, painfully, just out of reach,
then fleeing into the atmosphere.
The wordsmith still wilts in the woods
and his storytellers still declare
that those three words we long to hear
are mispronounced for all these years.

THE LACK THEREOF

To break
To be broken
To rebuild

What No One Understands About Clinical Depression

When you wake with such a weight on you
that your limbs are burdens you bear
and every time you try to raise your head,
you're combatted by the density of air;

When the breaths in your chest turn violent
and suddenly, you're a tornado touching down
and the words that spin and swirl in your wind
are of such a foreign sound;

When you must silence your storm,
and press on in the fight
because you can ruin the things you care most about
simply by ceasing to try;

When every ounce of your will is devoted to this,
how can one expect anything more?
And if the battle sees no end,
can you ever hope to win the war?

The Weight

The sound of snapping
The crunch of bones
Beneath the stones
That crush them
Against the ground
My limbs are pinned
Broken bits of rib
Dig into my lungs
I am breaking
But breathing
Waking
And seething
Waiting for the day
When the weight
Will have turned me
To diamond

Diamond's Blood

See through frosted windows.
Slash the gleaming glass!
Shards of crystal fall to snow,
Dye it red with diamond's blood.

Curse the damned illusions.
Cast away your mask!
Scattered specks of clarity,
Dye them red with diamond's blood.

The walking corpse of chivalry
Tips his tattered hat,
Shreds to pieces your perfect dress,
Dyes it red with diamond's blood.

My Demons & I

I am collateral damage,
the debris that is left after
my demons finish butting heads.
I lie in pieces, certain of one thing:
If I should lift the
shards,
specks,
and
slivers
of self
and find where they connect,
I would still feel fractured,
as if the lines of separation
had always existed,
casting only the illusion of a whole.

Either *Or*

Why am I always
either empty
or full;
boiling at the brim,
dangerously close to spilling,
or drained dry,
willing the filling
to start again?

I always feel
either flattened
or overinflated;
buzzing, almost bursting,
clinging to one breath,
or choked and gasping
for the next when the last
has left my lungs.

I am
either bottled
or broken;
seen through thick glass,
distorted by its curves,
or scattered everywhere,
edges glittering with light,
laid embarrassingly bare.

All-*Intrusive*

There's a monster in me
with no wish to be freed.
He just settles in deep
and says,
"You'll never be rid of me.
I'm in the blood that you bleed,
woven through your family,
and if I don't want you to know peace,
then that's one thing you'll never see."

The *Falling* Water

```
As the water trickles down my face,
it meets my tears and follows their
                        trace
                        and
                        the
                        one
                     place I
                  cannot hide
                now serves as my
                  disguise. The one
                place that exposes all
             is curtained in wall-to-wall
         and the falling water knows I'm dying
      because it's not for bathing but for crying.
```

The Midas Touch

King Midas, I am not.
Yet, when I have got
ahold of something,
it starts becoming
something new entirely
and it is easy, by early
in its transformation, to tell
what I have done to the thing I held.
Some have a green thumb and some gold.
But my story is yet untold.
The things I touch do not grow or gloss.
But, rather, melt down into chaos.

Voluntary Confinement

I built these walls around me
But I forgot to build a door
Now I sit hopelessly
On the cold hard floor
I am trapped
Wrapped in bricks
That soar to the sky
I know I am missing what lies beyond this room
But I've come to prefer confinement
Because every time I caved
Every time I cried
Everything I let happen
Every time I let you win
Every time I made myself lose
Every time I gave in
Everything I didn't choose
And every dream I never chased
All of it has been erased

No Doubt

When are you going to
break down that wall,
open the door,
and emerge?

I know that you feel broken, small.
But there is no one without worth.

We will be on the other side,
waiting to help you,
waiting for you to rise above pride and ask us to,
waiting for you to discover that recovering is possible.

And when, slowly,
the doorknob turns
and your head peeks out,
you will see us.

Have no doubt.

Who is She?

Who is she
trapped inside that frame?
She stares into my soul.

Why does she
share my eyes?
I'll bet she knows the things I know.

How does she
move just when I do?
I'd swear we're one and the same.

What would she
call herself?
I'll bet she'd whisper my name.

Where does she
go when I walk away,
out of her glassy view?

When did she become
a pile of pieces
in need of tending to?

I know the way she
must have felt
falling from her wall.

I think she may
hold the answer,
can I ever hang in the same hall?

I Hate the Word "I"

"I"

A concept that will make your eyes
run themselves dry; have you wondering,
"Why?" Why am I this way? Why is it so
difficult
to make it
through
`the day?
Why is
there so
much black
and white?
Why is
there no
gray? Will
"I" ever
be a
pleasant
term? I'm
not sure.
Is it
possible
to see
past the
horizon?
Will I ever find a grave to rest my lies on?
Will I ever tell myself the reasons for
the things I've done? I can only hope.

I Apologize

I can't believe you.
  I can't believe I finally did it!

How could you?
  How could I have waited so long?

You should know...
  I do.

You should have considered...
  I did.

It doesn't matter to you?
  It doesn't matter to you that I'm happy?

You shouldn't have done that.
  You shouldn't judge me, begrudge me my needs.

You should be ashamed of yourself.
  I have no reason to be ashamed of myself.

I'm sorry.

Why Am I Crying?

When I cry without a reason why
I almost wish something would kill me inside
So the tears would be justified

The Heat

My worst enemy; every day we have fought. It speaks silently. I stare into my own eyes. But I don't see myself. The mirrors multiply, swarm, and surround me. My face morphs into something sickening: my soul, it's slack from over-stretching. It's as if someone sparks a burner behind it. below my blood. How is this what I have become? The image fades, the mirrors condense, the glass reflects my face again. But the heat is still

Sense*less*

The words,
the words,
the words;
I know they're near.
I can sense them.
It is they who are senseless.

What is That Sound?

Head spinning
Sanity thinning
What is that sound?
Mind fumbling
Barriers crumbling
What is that sound?
The door creaks open
I step through
And recognize
That foreign noise
As truth

CROSSING

I am a perfectionist
      with an acquired taste
           for asymmetry.
                There's something in
                      the crossing of
                            chaos and beauty.

GAPS

I respect the gaps in my memory
for their efforts to protect me.
I could fight to fill them,
but I won't.

Pieced Together

When I was broken,
I thought
that I would never be whole again;
that I could only ever
be pieced together.

When I was healing,
I wondered
how much one can endure,
and where is the day when I can be more
than just pieced together?

Now that I am whole again,
I know
we are all broken and abstract,
connected at the cracks,
artfully pieced together.

The Tunnel

I know it's
terrifying
to look
within
yourself,
the dark
tunnel
that awaits.
And it'll
nearly kill
you, I know,
to allow
yourself
to feel
the weight
of your
mistakes
in the air.
You'll run
a hand,
blindly,
along the
wall as the
exit eludes
you. You'll
trip, and
fall, and
wonder if
you should
even get
back up
because
you can't
see what
would
happen
if you
could.
But I
promise
you, you
should
because
the light
at the
end of
the tunnel
is self-
-forgiveness
and it's
worth
every
damning
minute
in the
dark.

Flashing Lights

A light
Building as it burns
It flashes
The world freezes
And then
Just when
Everything is still
I see that I have reached
A place I'd only ever dreamed I'd be

I remember how it felt
How it sounded
The way it looked
The way it smelt
I remember everything about it
I remember far in the distance
Another light being lit

To *Pursue*

The pursuit of perfection
on which I've reflected before
from the perspective of the object;
I've since learned it is a fruitless pursuit.
I've since learned this point is moot.
I've since learned to pursue.

What Are You Writing For?

For me.
For my son.
For family.
For a world
with wet eyes,
heavy skies,
and empty hands.
For the falling
and the fallen.
For the breaking
and the broken.
For butterfly wing winds
and the rests in melodies.
For the things you can't see,
only feel on your cheeks.
For the scent of sugar
when it overwhelms a room.
For plot twists and jump scares
and crying vicariously.
For what lies below
and what flies above.
For hope.
For love.
And for the
lack thereof.

A Haiku for My Son

*My love for you is
the only thing to leave me
at a loss for words*

About the Author

Reese Landry is a Cuban-American writer living in Rhode Island. Her lifelong passion for writing has evolved into poetry, short fiction, and screenwriting that resonates with authenticity and emotional depth. She hopes her work will inspire unity and transformation in her readers. When Reese is not writing, she is a devoted mother to her son Daniel. Together they find joy in their shared adventures and the occasional impromptu dance party. Reese also spends time with her mother, Ana, who continues to be a steady source of love, encouragement and support.

Thank You for Reading
Hope, Love and The Lack Thereof
An Evolution of Mind

by Reese Landry

If you enjoyed reading this book, please consider leaving a review on your preferred platform. Your feedback supports quality content and helps inspire future releases.

Connect with the Author
reeselandrypoetry.com

 @reeselandrypoetry

Want the latest from the Brooklyn Writers Press?

Browse our Complete Catalog
brooklynwriterspress.com

www.ingramcontent.com/pod-product-compliance
Lightning Source LLC
Chambersburg PA
CBHW060527080526
44586CB00012B/647